Contents

Stage 7 Assessment

Written by
Alison Hawes

Illustrated by
Ollie Cuthbertson

Series editor **Dee Reid**

ALWAYS LEARNING

PEARSON

Before reading Haldor and the Dragon

Characters

Haldor

Larvig

A slave girl

Freya

New vocabulary

ch1 **p3** feasting	**ch3** **p14** staggered
ch1 **p4** nervously	**ch3** **p15** snatched
ch1 **p7** noticed	**ch3** **p17** spurted

Introduction

Years have passed and Haldor has become ruler of the kingdom. He has no son to rule after him but he has a daughter called Freya. One night, Haldor calls all his warriors to a feast in the Great Hall. He has something special to ask them. He wants Freya to become ruler after his death.

Haldor and the Dragon

Chapter One

Haldor and his warriors were feasting in the Great Hall. Haldor's old friend, Larvig, was seated on one side of him and Haldor's daughter, Freya, was on the other side.

Haldor stood up and spoke to the warriors.

"Tonight, let us honour my daughter, Freya," he said, "who one day I want to rule this kingdom after me."

Freya looked down and nervously twisted the new gold ring on her hand.

"This is not our way," whispered the warriors to
one another, "only great warriors can rule
this kingdom."
Suddenly the doors of the Great Hall burst open.
Four frightened men rushed in.

"Help us!" they shouted. "Our homes are on fire!"
Haldor and his warriors sprang to their feet and
rushed to help.

"What happened?" called Freya, as one of the

men ran past.

"It was a dragon!" he said.

When Freya heard this, her face turned as white as

the snow outside.

Through the open doors, she could see the huge flames as they rose high into the night sky and the strong warriors running to put them out. No one noticed her take off her gold ring and disappear into the dark night.

Chapter Two

The next morning, a slave girl noticed Freya had gone. She hurried to tell Haldor. Haldor asked everyone but no one had seen Freya.

Then the girl started crying, "I think I know where she is."

"Tell me!" Haldor yelled.

"About a month ago, Freya and I were out walking when there was a storm," explained the girl. "We hid in a cave to get out of the rain. But it was a dragon's cave. It was full of gold."

"As we left," the girl went on, "Freya picked up a gold sword. She wanted to take it home to give to you. But I was worried the dragon would wake and see the sword had gone. I was frightened he would kill us all."

"So did she take it?" asked Haldor.

"No," said the slave girl, "But…"

"But what?" roared Haldor.

"I saw Freya put a gold ring in her pocket.
Maybe she thought the dragon attacked
the people because she had taken the ring.
I think she has gone to return it."

Haldor grabbed his sword. "Take me there now!"

he shouted. "Quick, before it's too late!"

Chapter Three

The girl led Haldor to the cave.

"Wait here!" he said, then slipped into the cave.

Haldor could hear Freya crying. The dragon had her by the neck.

"I have returned the ring. Now let me go!" she begged.

"Never!" roared the dragon. "I will kill you for taking my ring."

Haldor hit the dragon with his sword. It staggered against the cave wall and let go of Freya.

"Run!" Haldor yelled at his daughter.

Freya ran from the cave. Haldor pushed his sword
hard into the dragon's neck. But the sword hit
bone and snapped in half. The dragon roared and
snatched Haldor around the throat.

Freya heard her father scream.

"Find Larvig," she told the slave girl. "Quick,

before it's too late!"

Freya slipped into the cave. The dragon was

slowly crushing the life out of Haldor.

Freya's heart filled with anger. She lifted the
dragon's gold sword and with a mighty roar
pushed it deep into its body. Blood spurted from
the wound. Both the dragon and Haldor fell to
the floor.

Freya rushed to where her father lay and held him
in her arms. "Don't die, Father!" she whispered.
But it was already too late.

Chapter Four

The warriors brought Haldor's body back to the Great Hall and Larvig spoke to them all. "Haldor has no warrior son," he said, "so he wanted Freya to rule after him. I heard you say she is no warrior, but she killed the dragon just like any great warrior."

"This is true," agreed the warriors.

Later, Freya and Larvig walked behind her warriors
as they carried Haldor's body on to his ship.

"You killed the dragon, Freya," Larvig said. "That
gold is yours."

"I don't want it," said Freya. "I killed the dragon
to try and save my father. I didn't do it for
the gold. I will give the gold to those who
were attacked by the dragon."

"Then just keep this," said Larvig and he gave Freya the gold ring she had taken all those weeks before.

"No!" said Freya, "It will only remind me of the terrible mistake I made!"

"That is why you should keep it for ever," he said. "It will make you rule better."

Freya knew Larvig spoke the truth and put the ring in her pocket.

Then she and Larvig watched as the wind carried Haldor and his dragon boat over the sea and far away into the distance.

Quiz

p5 Why did the four men burst into the Great Hall?
   a) They wanted to join the feast.
   b) Their homes were on fire.
   c) The warriors were whispering to one another.

p8 Why did the slave girl speak to Haldor?
   a) She thought she knew where Freya had gone.
   b) She wanted to ask Haldor where Freya had gone.
   c) She was afraid of Haldor.

p11 What did Freya take from the dragon's cave?
   a) A gold sword.
   b) A gold cup.
   c) A gold ring.

p15 Why did Haldor's sword not kill the dragon?
   a) The sword hit bone and snapped in half.
   b) Haldor did not push the sword hard enough.
   c) Haldor was afraid of the dragon.

p18 Why did the warriors let Freya become their ruler?
   a) They didn't think a woman should be ruler.
   b) Freya killed the dragon like a great warrior.
   c) They wanted Larvig to be ruler.

Inferential comprehension

p4 Why did Freya nervously twist the gold ring on her hand?

p5 Why did the warriors say 'This is not our way'?

p20 Why does Larvig say keeping the gold ring will make Freya a better ruler?

- How does Freya prove she is a great warrior?

- Are there any clues that show the slave girl is brave?

Personal response

- Do you think Freya should have taken the gold ring?

- Would you have gone back to the dragon's cave to return the ring?

- Do you think Freya will be a good ruler?

- Can women be just as good rulers as men?

Published by Pearson Education Limited, Edinburgh Gate, Harlow, Essex, CM20 2JE.

www.pearsonschoolsandfecolleges.co.uk

Text © Pearson Education Limited 2012

Edited by Ruth Emm
Designed by Siu Hang Wong
Original illustrations © Pearson Education Limited 2012
Illustrated by Ollie Cuthbertson
Cover design by Siu Hang Wong

Cover illustration © Pearson Education Limited 2012

The right of Alison Hawes to be identified as author of this work has been asserted by her in
accordance with the Copyright, Designs and Patents Act 1988.

First published 2012

Fourteenth impression, 2023

British Library Cataloguing in Publication Data
A catalogue record for this book is available from the British Library

ISBN 978 0 435 07163 9

Printed in Great Britain by Ashford Colour Press Ltd.